W9-AHA-753

TOOLS FOR TEACHERS

- **ATOS:** 0.6
- **GRL:** D
- **WORD COUNT:** 32

- **CURRICULUM CONNECTIONS:** emotions

Skills to Teach

- **HIGH-FREQUENCY WORDS:** a, he, her, him, his, is, it, she, the, with, you
- **CONTENT WORDS:** afraid, dark, face, hides, light, scares, sleeps, spider
- **PUNCTUATION:** exclamation point, periods, question marks
- **WORD STUDY:** long /a/ spelled ai (*afraid*); long /e/, spelled ee (*sleeps*)
- **TEXT TYPE:** information report

Before Reading Activities

- Read the title and give a simple statement of the main idea.
- Have students "walk" though the book and talk about what they see in the pictures.
- Introduce new vocabulary by having students predict the first letter and locate the word in the text.
- Discuss any unfamiliar concepts that are in the text.

After Reading Activities

The book's text mentions some situations or things that may cause fear. Ask the children if they have something that scares them. Do they face their fears? How? Maybe they have already overcome some fears. Ask children to draw a fear they have. Have them pair up with a friend. Each child should show their fear to their partner and explain their fear. If they don't have an idea for overcoming their fear, ask them to ask their partner for ideas.

Tadpole Books are published by Jump!, 5357 Penn Avenue South, Minneapolis, MN 55419, www.jumplibrary.com

Copyright ©2019 Jump. International copyright reserved in all countries. No part of this book may be reproduced in any form without written permission from the publisher.

Editor: Jenna Trnka   **Designer:** Anna Peterson

Photo Credits: Patrick Foto/Shutterstock, cover; Juanmonino/iStock, 1; Maria Taglienti-Molinari/Getty, 2–3, 16tl; Radka Palenikova/Shutterstock, 4–5 (spider); Dennie Cody and Duangkamon Khattiya/Getty, 4–5 (boy), 16tm; Realstock/Shutterstock, 6–7, 10–11, 16tr, 16bm, 16br; Ian Andreiev/Dreamstime, 8–9 (hand); epantha/iStock, 8–9 (spider); dmitro2009/Shutterstock, 12–13; kali9/iStock, 14–15, 16bl.

Library of Congress Cataloging-in-Publication Data
Names: Nilsen, Genevieve.
Title: Afraid / by Genevieve Nilsen.
Description: Tadpole Edition. | Minneapolis, MN : Jump!, Inc., (2018) | Series: Emotions | Includes index.
Identifiers: LCCN 2018006012 (print) | LCCN 2017061686 (ebook) | ISBN 9781624969454 (ebook) |
ISBN 9781624969430 (hardcover : alk. paper) | ISBN 9781624969447 (pbk.)
Subjects: LCSH: Fear. | Emotions.
Classification: LCC BF575.F2 (print) | LCC BF575.F2 N55 2018 (ebook) | DDC 152.4/6—dc23
LC record available at https://lccn.loc.gov/2018006012

EMOTIONS

AFRAID

by Genevieve Nilsen

TABLE OF CONTENTS

tadpole
books

AFRAID

She is afraid.

spider

A spider scares him.

He covers his face.

The dark scares her.

She hides.

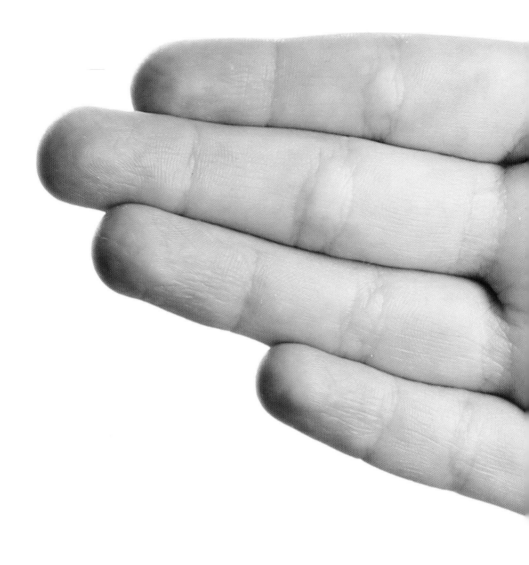

He holds a spider.

light

She sleeps with a light.

What scares you?

Try it!

WORDS TO KNOW

afraid covers dark

hides light spider

INDEX